WRITE LIKE A HIGH SCHOOLER

Your Step-by-Step Writing practice

BY

Lacaarj Stationery

Book name: Write like a High Schooler

Book cover designed by: Lois Cole

Book layout: Lois Cole

Illustrator: Gregory Brown & Umer Zulfiqar

Self-published: Lacaarj Stationery

Email address: sales@lacaarjstationery.com

Printed in: USA

National Library of Jamaica Cataloguing in Publication Data

Author: Lois Cole

ISBN: 978-976-97256-1-4

Preface

The purpose of creating this book was to offer a practical resource for anyone eager to explore the realm of writing in the real world. Writing isn't just about crafting stories or essays; it's an essential skill used in various aspects of life. This book covers a wide array of writing topics relevant to everyday situations, including composing letters, engaging in debates, expressing complaints, sharing accomplishments, composing reviews and much more.

The decision to include diverse topics stems from the belief that a well-rounded writer should effectively express themselves in any situation. My objective in creating this book is simple: to provide practical guidance and inspiration for students, aspiring writers, and anyone seeking support in their writing endeavors.

This book is structured to guide you or your child systematically through various learning levels, offering step-by-step instructions and guided practice. It serves as a versatile tool for classrooms, complementing teachers' instruction and pedagogy. Furthermore, parents can utilize this book for homeschooling, homework assistance, end-of-term/year examinations, and summer holiday exercises to ensure preparedness for the upcoming school year.

Upon completing this book successfully, your child should be able to demonstrate critical thinking skills, implement brainstorming techniques, follow instructions correctly, observe desired strategies and behaviors, and become more confident in the subject matter. I envision this book as a reliable companion, fostering proficient communication in diverse real-world scenarios.

Table of Contents

Introduction

Welcome to the world of writing, where words come to life in various exciting forms. Imagine sending invitations that make people eager to join your party, engaging in debates where you express your thoughts passionately, and crafting stories – some real, some imaginary – in fiction and non-fiction. Picture yourself writing heartfelt letters to friends or important business letters that make things happen. Dive into the rhythm of poetry, where words dance like music, and explore the art of sharing your opinions through reviews. This magical world of writing is your canvas, and with every stroke of the pen, you have the power to create, express, and make your mark in countless ways!

8 Tips to Improve Your Child's Writing Skills:

1. Read regularly and repeatedly.
2. Stick to a consistent reading routine.
3. Make reading and writing enjoyable and engaging.
4. Practice writing every day.
5. Encourage jotting down thoughts and ideas.
6. Foster connections between what is read and personal experiences or other texts.
7. Create a dedicated writing space conducive to creativity.
8. Provide positive encouragement and praise to boost confidence in writing endeavors.

LETTER WRITING

Letter writing is when you write a message to someone on paper or using a computer. You write to share your thoughts, feelings, or information in a structured way, like with greetings and closings. People write letters to talk to friends and family, say thank you, or even talk to businesses or authorities. Even though we don't write letters as much as before because of emails and texts, it's still an important skill. It helps us be clear, understanding, and connected when we write to others.

Informal – Friendly letter Layout

(Heading) ⟶

(Senders address and date)

2 Malcolm Way

St. James

Jamaica

July 1, 2019

Dear Kerry,

⟵ (Greetings)

(The person whom you are writing to)

How are you doing?

(Indent)   means starting away from the margin

Body of the letter

Your Friend, ⟵ (Closing)

Jessica ⟵ (Signature)

Sample Letter

12 Queens way

St. James

Jamaica

January 10, 2019

Dear Ashley,

      I hope you are doing well. I am thrilled to write this letter to tell you about my trip to Disneyland this summer vacation. The moment I stepped into the enchanting world of Disney, I was greeted by a lively parade of my favourite characters, including Donald Duck and Mickey Mouse. The atmosphere was filled with pure magic, and I felt like I had stepped into a fairy tale.

      Without a doubt, Disneyland is one of the happiest place on earth for everyone. From thrilling rides like the flying elephant and Peter Pan flight to the captivating 4D movie theater, every moment was filled with wonder and adventure. I even had the chance to explore the majestic Sleeping Beauty castle and embark on the Jungle Cruise, a thrilling expedition through the heart of Disney's wild wonders.

      Finally, I got to meet my favorite Disney characters, interact with them, and capture some unforgettable photographs. I couldn't resist bringing back souvenirs for you and my other friends too. I must say, it was one of the best trips of my life. This mesmerizing trip has inspired me, and I think we should plan a friend's trip to Disneyland next summer. It would be an incredible experience to share the magic and joy of Disneyland with you.

Your friend,

Brad

How I Spent My Summer Holiday

✔ I wrote the heading.

✔ I wrote the greetings.

✔ I wrote the body (beginning with an indented margin). **1st par.**

✔ I expressed my happiness to hear that she is doing well.

✔ I informed her of the purpose behind my letter.

✔ I shared my vivid thoughts and impressions about Disneyland.

✔ I describe the magical atmosphere, interactions with the beloved characters and how I felt.

✔ I shared my perspectives on who Disneyland caters for. **2nd par.**

✔ I shared the thrilling rides, amusements, and adventures at Disneyland, describing all the fun things I explored.

✔ I shared the joy of meeting our beloved Disney characters, and capturing those unforgettable moments in photos. **3rd par.**

✔ I informed her about the souvenirs I brought back and for whom.

✔ I expressed my feelings after the Disneyland visit.

✔ I suggested planning a friend's trip to Disneyland next summer.

✔ I concluded the letter by expressing my excitement about sharing the magic and joy of Disneyland together and signed it with my signature.

Letter to a Friend

> <u>Note</u>: Friendly letter is a type of letter written to persons who are your relatives, friends, peers, acquaintances, or anyone with whom you have a relationship with.

<u>Instructions:</u>

1. Write a friendly letter to your friend, sharing your first day's experience in a sport or hobby you enjoyed.

2. Use the writing guide to structure your letter.

2 **Sample Guide**

Getting Started:

✔ Write the heading: Write the recipient's address and date.

✔ Warm Greetings: Open your letter with a friendly greeting.

Engaging Introduction: 1st par.

✔ Write the body: Begin with an indentation and something captivating – a question, a surprising fact, or a statement setting the scene.

✔ Sport or Hobby details: Describe the specific sport or hobby in detail. For example, if it's soccer, talk about the field, the ball, and the players.

✔ Emotions: Share your feelings from the first day. Did you feel excited, nervous, or confident?

✔ Atmosphere: Describe the atmosphere of the place. Was it noisy, peaceful, energetic, or competitive?

Unveiling the Experience: 2nd par.

✔ Activities: Discuss the activities you participated in, such as passing, shooting, or practicing drills. Explain how you felt throughout the day.

✔ People: Describe the people you met. Were they friendly, supportive, or competitive?

✔ Challenges: Talk about any challenges faced and how you overcame them, like learning a new move or adapting to the game.

✔ Victories: Talk about any achievements, whether it was scoring a goal, making a new friend, or mastering a skill.

✔ Overall Experience: Summarize your entire experience. Did you enjoy it? Was it as expected?

Connecting on a Personal Level: 3rd par.

✔ Returning to one's abode: Mentioned who accompanied you home after the sports or hobby session.

 Invite Friend's Experience: Encourage your friend to share their own experiences. Ask questions to make the conversation feel interactive and engaging.

Closing on a Friendly Note: 4th par.

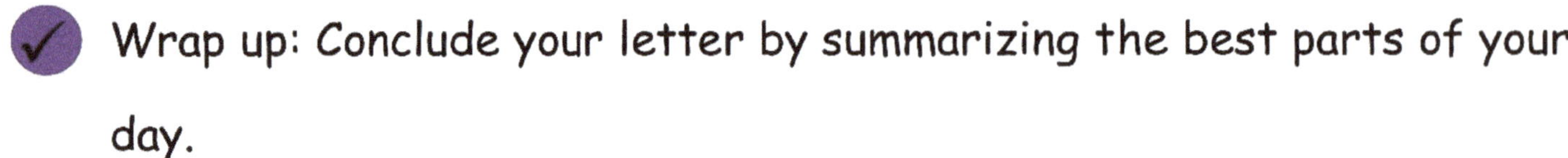 Wrap up: Conclude your letter by summarizing the best parts of your day.

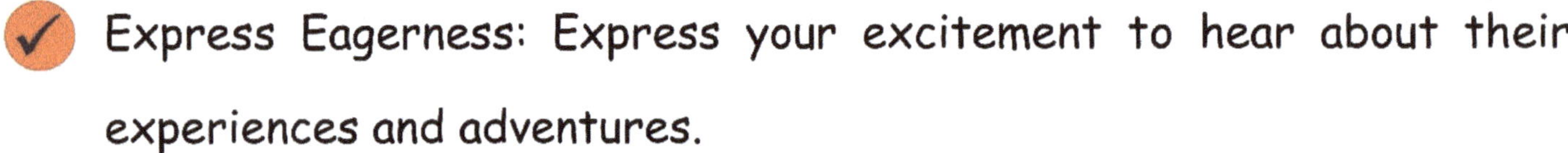 Express Eagerness: Express your excitement to hear about their experiences and adventures.

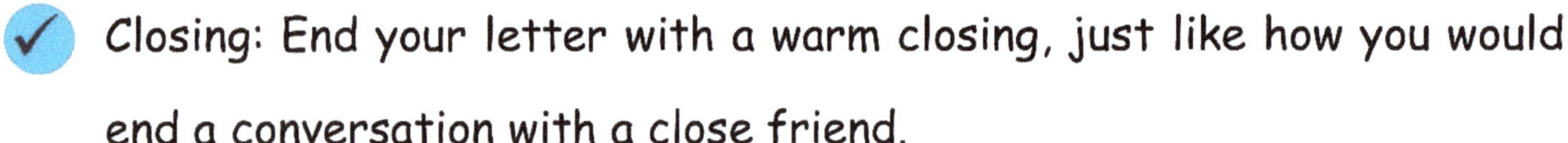 Closing: End your letter with a warm closing, just like how you would end a conversation with a close friend.

Get Well Soon

<u>Instructions:</u>

1. Write a get-well soon letter to someone you know that is sick.

2. Use the writing guide to structure your letter.

3 Writing Guide

✔ Write the heading.

✔ Write the greetings.

✔ Begin the body (Start with an indentation from the margin).

✔ Write a sentence indicating that you know about their illness.

✔ Write something that will motivate him/her to continue fighting to get well.

✔ Offer your assistance in any way you can.

✔ Share with them what you think might help them recover faster.

✔ Ask their permission to visit him/her.

✔ Write a prayer or a positive though expressing your hope for their swift recovery.

✔ Close your letter and sign it.

Apology Letter

<u>Instructions:</u>

1. Write a letter to your best friend apologizing to him or her for something you have done.

2. Use the writing guide to structure your letter.

- ✔ Write the heading.
- ✔ Write the greetings.
- ✔ Begin the (start with an indent from the margin).
- ✔ Write an acknowledgement statement, explaining that you understand what you are apologizing for.
- ✔ Describe your feelings before and after the incident and why you behaved the way you did.
- ✔ Express genuine remorse for your actions and demonstrate that you understand how your friend felt.
- ✔ Offer to take steps to make amends.
- ✔ Clearly express what you hope for in the future of your friendship.
- ✔ Close your letter and sign it.

Thank You letter

> **Note:** A thank you letter is used when one person or party wishes to express appreciation to another.

Instructions:

1. Write a letter to a parent or grandparent to express your gratitude for everything they've done for you.

2. Use the writing guide to structure your letter

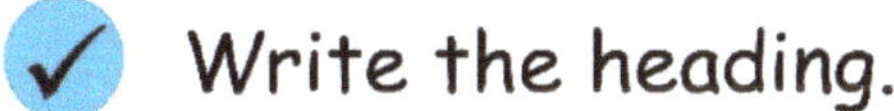

5 Writing Guide

- ✔ Write the heading.
- ✔ Write the greetings.
- ✔ Write the body (Start with an indentation from the margin).
- ✔ Start the body of your letter with a statement of gratitude, using words like "incredible grateful" or "eternally thankful."
- ✔ Write the things you are thankful for. Reflect on their presence, teachings, or even the comfort of their cuddles.
- ✔ Share a cherished memory of an activity you did together and explain why that moment was special to you.
- ✔ Close your letter with a heartfelt conclusion and your signature.

Sample Achievement Letter

24 Miller Drive

St. Andrew

Jamaica

March 9, 2020

Dear Mom,

I hope this letter finds you both in good health and high spirits. I am thrilled to share some wonderful news with you! Can you guess what the highest grade on my report card is? Well, I'm delighted to inform you that I achieved the highest grade possible, an 'A'! I am filled with pride and excitement over this accomplishment.

This achievement means a great deal to me because it reflects the hard work I've put in throughout the year. I dedicated myself to studying for tests, sought help from my teachers whenever necessary, and consistently strived to do my best. Earning an 'A' fills me with confidence, showing me that I can achieve anything with determination.

Mom and Dad, I want to express my heartfelt gratitude to both of you for your steadfast support and encouragement. Your belief in me has been a constant source of motivation, and I am deeply thankful for it. I promise to continue working hard and striving for excellence, always aiming to make you proud.

Your son,

Stewart

Achievement Letter

Instructions

1. Write a friendly letter to a parent telling them about your latest report card and the things you're proud of achieving.

2. Use the writing guide to structure your letter

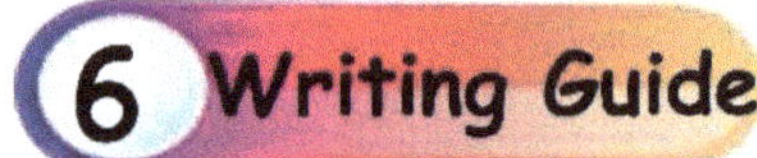

6 Writing Guide

✔ Write the heading.

✔ Write the greetings.

✔ Write the body. (Start with an indent from the margin).

✔ Write a sentence to express well wishes or a concern.

✔ Write an Attention-Grabbing statement or question to express the news you are about to share.

✔ In a sentence express the highest grade you achieved and describe how it makes you feel.

✔ Explain why this achievement means a lot to you.

✔ Describe the steps you took to prepare for achieving those grades.

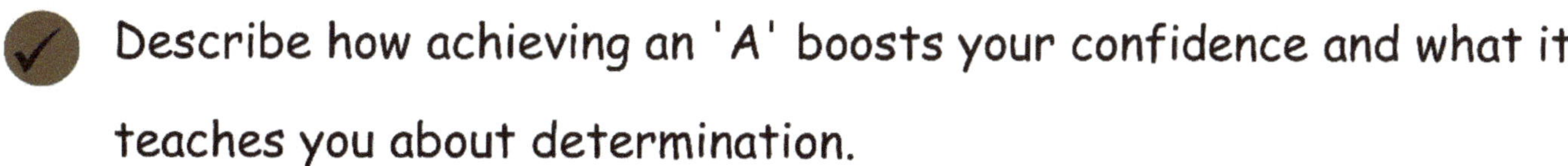

✔ Describe how achieving an 'A' boosts your confidence and what it teaches you about determination.

✔ Thank your parents for always believing in you and keeping you motivated.

✔ Commit to continuing your efforts and striving to do your best in order to make your parents proud.

✔ Close your letter and sign it with your signature.

Party Invitation

<u>Instructions:</u>

1. Write a party invitation to friends or family inviting them to a special event. Fill in the provided blank spaces.

Party Invitation

Dear, ___________________________

____

You are invited to my _______________

I am feeling ____________ and __________

to celebrate with you at ________ o'clock.

____

The event will take place at ___________

____

Your parents should pick you up at ________ o'clock.

____

Please confirm by ____________ at the latest to

Inform me know if you'll be able to attend.

____

____

Your friend, ________________________

____

It's a party

Formal – Business Letter Layout

(Heading) ⟶
(Sender's address and date)

2 Malcolm Way
St. James
Jamaica
July 1, 2019

The Manager   ⟵ (Recipient's Details)
Bebras Company   (The person whom you are writing to)
2 Karr Crescent
St. James
Jamaica

Dear Sir/Madam,   ⟵ (Greetings)

    My name is Jason Myer's, from Little Angel's Academy…

(Indent)

Body of the letter

Yours faithfully,   ⟵ (Closing)
Jason Myer's   ⟵ (Signature)
Little Angel's Academy

Sample Enquiry Letter

15 Malcolm Drive

St. James

Jamaica

December 10, 2019

The Manager

Bebras Company

10 Church street

St. James

Jamaica

Dear Mr. Clark,

 I am Jason Myers, representing Little Angel's Academy in Kingston. I am writing to inquire about the Bebras Sponsorship program recently advertised on television.

 Our school has been actively seeking a computer science program to integrate into our curriculum. After thorough research, we found that your program aligns perfectly with our educational goals. To proceed with our application, we need additional details to ensure a complete understanding of the program's requirements and to facilitate the sponsorship process.

 I would greatly appreciate receiving more details on the age group eligibility, opening and closing times, package inclusions, and costs associated with the program. I eagerly await your response.

Yours faithfully,

Jason Myers

Little Angel's Academy

Business Letter of Enquiry

> **Note:** These types of letter are sent when you want to ask a business for more information about a service or product.

Instructions:

1. Use the writing guide to draft a letter to the manager of your chosen amusement park, requesting information about their children's package.

2. Use the writing guide to structure your letter.

7 Writing Guide

- ✔ Write the heading.
- ✔ Write the recipient's details
- ✔ Write the greetings.
- ✔ Start the body of the letter with an indent.
- ✔ Introduce yourself and mention your current school affiliation.
- ✔ Explain the purpose of your letter, indicating where you saw their advertisement.
- ✔ Describe how the park caught your attention and why it is relevant.
- ✔ Clarify what information or action you are seeking.
- ✔ Request the Information and be specific about the details you are seeking. Express Your Anticipation.
- ✔ Close your letter and sign it.

Business Letter of Request

<u>Instructions:</u>

1. Write a business letter addressed to your school principal requesting to have a STEM program integrated into the school curriculum.
2. Use the writing guide to structure your letter.

8 Writing Guide

✔ Write the heading and the recipient's details.

✔ Start with a polite greeting, addressing the principal respectfully.

✔ Begin the body of your letter with an indent.

✔ Introduce yourself, mentioning your name and current grade.

✔ Clearly state why you're writing and express why you want the STEM program in your school curriculum.

✔ State a question or an interesting fact to persuade your principal.

✔ State some advantages of having a STEM program at your school.

✔ State how your request could benefit the students in the future.

✔ State what you would like your principal to do about your request.

✔ State how the principal can locate you if he or she has more questions regarding your request.

✔ Close your letter and sign it.

"Thank you" Business Letter

Note: These types of letter are sent when you want to thank an organization or someone.

Instructions:

1. Write a thank-you letter to the cruise ship manager for hosting your class on the field trip and making it enjoyable.

2. Use the writing guide structure your letter.

9 Writing Guide

✔ Write the heading and the receiver's details.

✔ Greetings: Start your letter with a polite salutation.

✔ Begin the body of your letter with an indent from the margin.

✔ Introduce yourself by stating your name and the school you attend.

✔ Write a sincere thank you sentence expressing your gratitude for the enjoyable trip. Mention how much you enjoyed the visit.

✔ Provide examples of what you particularly enjoyed about the trip. You can mention things like the ship tour, the use of the telescope, or any other remarkable moments.

✔ Close your letter warmly and professionally. Sign it with your name.

Business Letter of Complaint

> <u>Note:</u> These types of letters are sent when someone has done something wrong, or you want to make a complaint about a product or service.

<u>Instructions:</u>

1. Write a letter to the manager at Delicious Beef Patty complaining about the long lines caused by having only one cashier.

2. Use the writing guide to structure your letter.

✔ Write the heading.

✔ Write the receiver's details.

✔ Write the greetings.

✔ Begin the body with an indent from the margin.

✔ Introduce yourself briefly and explain the purpose of your letter.

✔ Include details of the date and time when the issue happened.

✔ Mention the problem: long lines due to only one cashier.

✔ Offer a suggestion on how they can improve their service.

✔ Explain why you believe your suggestion would enhance the customer experience. Express your anticipation for resolution.

✔ Close your letter and sign it.

Answer the Letter-Writing Questions

1. What does it mean to begin a paragraph with an indentation from the margin? ____

2. How does a business letter of inquiry differ from a business letter of request? ____
____

3. What specific information should you include when writing the receiver's details in your letter? ____
____

4. How does a business letter differ from a friendly letter in terms of content and tone? ____
____

5. Can you provide one reason why someone might write a complaint letter to a company? ____
____

6. What details or information should be included in the heading of your letter? ____
____

Figurative Language

Writers use figurative language to make stories more exciting and colourful. Instead of just saying things plainly, they use imaginative words and comparisons to paint a vivid picture in your mind. It helps you feel the emotions of the characters and imagine the scenes in a livelier way, making the story more interesting and fun to read.

Hyperbole Story

Hisham and his sister

> **Definition:** A hyperbole is a figure of speech where you describe something in an exaggerated manner, making it sound much bigger or more extreme than it really is.
>
> **Example:** I was so hungry that I could eat an entire mountain.

Instruction:

1. Read the guided prompts and the story below to understand how the prompts are used to construct a story.

Story Summary

This story will be about Hisham and his sister who are very tired from trekking in the mountains. They come across a little hut where an old lady offers them water to drink.

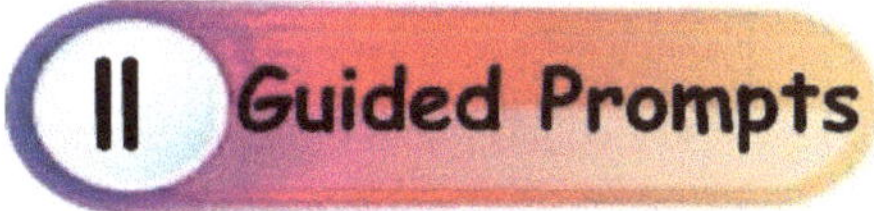

Line 1-2: You can start by writing about what Hisham and his sister were doing (in this case, trekking in the mountains). When did they start walking?

Example: *Hisham and his sister were trekking in the mountains. They set off from their camp early in the morning.*

Line 2-4: What time is it now? Think of a way you can convey how much time has passed. How were they feeling after walking for so long? How can you exaggerate this feeling?

Example: *Now, the sun was high up in the sky. They were so thirsty that they felt they could empty an entire ocean.*

Line 4-5: While trekking, you need to carry your stuff in your own bag. How would you feel if you had to walk for so long with a heavy bag? How can you emphasize this?

Example: *Their bags felt as heavy as mountains, and they struggled to move ahead.*

Line 5-7: When you walk for a long time, do you have shortness of breath? How can this be emphasize using hyperbole? When they are struggling so much to keep walking, they might be thinking of giving up. But suddenly, they come across something that gives them hope. What could this be?

Example: Each breath they took stung like needles in their throat. *Just as they were about to give up, they saw a small hut ahead of them.*

Line 7-8: What else do they see? Was the hut empty or was there anyone in the hut? Can you think of a hyperbole to emphasize this?

Example: *There was a woman seated in front of the hut who looked even older than the mountains.*

Line 8-9: When you see an old person's face, what is usually the most distinguishing feature? Have you noticed that old people have many wrinkles on their face? how can you exaggerate the number of wrinkles on this old woman's face?

Example: *There were more lines of age on her face than blades of grass on the meadow.*

Line 10: Now, you can add a contrasting feature to describe the old lady. Usually, such an old lady would look more somber and sullen. Try to use a hyperbole to emphasize her smile.

Example: *But her joyful face was framed by a smile that was a mile wide.*

Line 11-12: Would Hisham and his sister approach the hut? As the old lady sees them, tired and thirsty, what does she do?

Example: *As Hisham and his sister approached the hut, the old lady got up and offered them water to drink.*

Line 12-13: *How does this water feel to the tired and thirsty travelers? Use a hyperbole to describe how they fell about this water?*

Example: *Tired as they were, the water felt more full of life than the most potent elixir in the world.*

Hisham and his sister

L1 Hisham and his sister were trekking in the mountains. They set off

L2 from their camp early in the morning. Now, the sun was high up

L3 in the sky. They were so thirsty, they felt they could drink an

L4 entire ocean. Their bags felt as heavy as mountains, and they

L5 struggled to move ahead. Each breath they took stung like

L6 needles in their throat. But just as they were about to give up,

L7 they saw a small hut. There was a woman seated in front of the

L8 hut who looked even older than the mountains. Her face showed

L9 more lines of age than there were blades of grass in a meadow.

L10 But her joyful face was framed by a smile that was a mile wide.

L11 As Hisham and his sister approached the hut, the old lady got up

L12 and offered them water to drink. Tired as they were, the water

L13 felt more full of life than the most potent elixir in the world.

Activity: Read the questions below and use a marker to highlight the hyperbolic answers in the story above.

1. How thirsty were Hisham and his sister as they trekked through the mountains?

2. How heavy did their bags feel as they struggled to move forward?

3. How intense was the sensation of each breath they took?

Hyperbole Story

The Dense Jungle of Indonesia

Instructions:

1. Follow the guided prompts to write a hyperbole story based on the summary below.

2. Use describing or sound words (i.e., *swish* or *slush*).

Story summary

Paul was exploring the dense jungles of Indonesia, looking for an ancient palace. He was extremely tired from slashing through the forest. Finally, he came across a clearing and found the ancient palace standing in front of him. He broke down in tears.

12 Guided Prompts

1 **Start with a scene that grabs attention:** Describe what Paul was doing in the dense forest using words about walking. When did he begin his journey?

2 **Explore Paul's emotions:** Show his distress, the ache in his arms from cutting through plants. Use strong words to highlight his tiredness. Imagine how this exhaustion affected his feelings.

3 **Illustrate Paul's intense hunger using exaggerated language:** Make his desperation for food clear. Describe it as if he could eat a huge feast in one gulp. Introduce the idea of a fever, making it seem very intense.

4 **Explain Paul's reason for being in the forest:** What brought him there? Was it a search for treasure, history, or a personal mission? Clarify his goals and what he hoped to find in the wilderness.

5 **Discuss the importance of the place:** Why was this location special? Did legends mention its mystical powers, or was it linked to his past? Use expressive words to highlight the extraordinary nature of this spot.

6 **Describe the key moment when Paul discovers the ancient palace:** What emotions did he feel? Was he amazed, relieved, or in disbelief? Capture his immediate reaction as he realizes the significance of his discovery.

7 **Create a vivid image of the ancient palace:** Exaggerate its age and grandeur. How did its architecture stand out in the wild? Use detailed descriptions to transport readers to this remarkable setting.

8 **Convey Paul's overwhelming emotions after finding what he sought:** Was he full of joy, gratitude, or mixed feelings? Exaggerate his reaction, describing tears flowing like rivers to show the depth of his emotions. Make this moment intense to connect with readers.

Alliteration Story

> **Definition:** When two or more words in a row start with the same sound.
> **Example:** 1. Sally sells seashells by the seashore.
>   2. The sunset created a stunning scene.

Instructions:

1. Read the story below and list all the alliteration words in each row to demonstrate your understanding.

2. Compose a brief alliteration story of your own.

Bella woke up to the merry melody of morning birds. It was a delightful day. She was at her Nana's farm for her holidays. Bella joyfully jumped out of the bed and swiftly sprinted out into the sunshine. She could see her Nana milking Jenny, the cute charming cow. Bella bent down and kissed her Nana. She chased the beautiful butterflies all over the green grass. The bumblebees buzzed as they flew from one flower to another. Finally, Nana called out for breakfast. Bella rushed inside to see a bowl of savory steaming soup, freshly baked buns and a beautiful block of butter waiting for her at the table.

Simile Story

> **Definition:** It's like when you say, "She's as brave as a lion." You're comparing someone to a lion to show how brave they are, even though they're not really a lion.

Izzy and her Grandpa

Instructions:

Follow the guided prompts to write your own story based on the summary below. Use similes as described above, where appropriate.

Story Summary

Izzy and her grandpa lived in the mountains. One day, Izzy came across a strange glowing stone. As she held it, the surface broke apart and a baby dragon emerged from it.

13 Guided Prompts

1. Start with where Izzy and her grandpa lived. Use adjective or adverbs for the reader to visualize it.

②   Write about something that they were doing right before Izzy finds something. What does she find? Where was it hidden?

3   Izzy was attracted to this strange object. Find a simile that can be used to describe someone uncontrollably attracted to someone or something.

4   Izzy must have been curious. What did she do? What did she notice when she picked it up? You can describe this strange object using similes.

5   What was its shape? Was it rough or smooth?

6   Was it cold or warm? Was there anything special about it?

7   Izzy noticed numerous lines on its surface. Express what could this be compared to?

8   Did the object undergo any change as Izzy held it? Can you describe what happened?

9   What kind of creature emerged from this strange looking object? Write about a feature that helped Izzy identify this creature.

10   What did Izzy realize about the strange object and the creature that emerged from it?

Personification Story

> **Definition:** Personification gives human qualities and traits to non-human entities or objects. For example, "The wind whispered through the trees."

Instructions

1. Rewrite The Mama cactus story. Replace the underlined words and phrases with synonyms or alternative expressions from the list below.

2. Use a dictionary for unfamiliar words.

• other flora might have	• appeared unhappy
• succulent cactus	• Why do I appear so unattractive?
• thorns shielded the cactus	• lovely foliage
• prickly spines	• fragile and tender stems
• ravenous and parched	• dance in the breeze
• approach me	• habitat is incredibly arid
• withered due to thirst	• If we possessed numerous leaves
• valuable your thorns prove to be	• Dehydrated
• succumbed	• stood shoulder to shoulder
• sturdy limbs	

The Mama Cactus

The Mama and baby cactus <u>stood side-by-side</u> on the endless sandy desert. The baby cactus <u>looked sad</u>. He asked his mama, "<u>Why do I look so ugly?</u> None of the other plants <u>come near me</u> because of my thorns. The other trees have such beautiful leaves to <u>play in the air</u>. But I have only <u>spiny thorns</u>. While the other trees have <u>strong branches</u>, we have only these <u>soft and squishy stems</u>." The Mama cactus smiled and pointed to a nearby tree that had <u>dried from the want of water</u>. "Our <u>home is so dry</u>. <u>If we had so many leaves</u>, we would <u>dry out</u> just like that tree over there" she said. Just then a fox came along, <u>hungry and thirsty</u>. It tried to feed on the <u>fleshy cactus</u>, but the <u>thorns protected the cactus</u> from being eaten. Mama cactus silently smiled at baby cactus and said, "you see how <u>useful your thorns are</u>, <u>other plants would have been defeated</u>, because they have no thorns to protect them.

Onomatopoeia Story

<u>Instructions</u>

1. Fill in the blanks in the 'Beach Day Adventure' story with appropriate onomatopoeia words from the blue column.

2. Create your own onomatopoeia story titled 'Adventure in the Jungle' using the words from the pink column.

• CLINK CLANK SLAM THUD!	• SNAP!
• SWISH.	• SLIP!
• BEEP BEEP BEEP BEEP!	• CREEEAK!
• ZOOM!	• TAP TAP TAP!
• ZIP!	• RUMBLE!
• WOOHOO!	• SWOOSH!
• SPLASH!	• CLICK CLICK!
• SCREEEEECH!	

The Beach Day Adventure

_______________________________________ The alarm went off. As Daisy snoozed the alarm, she was already very happy. _______________________________ It's Sunday today," she thought, a day without school and studies. _______________________________ She opened her window curtains to look out into the sunny Sunday morning. They were going to the beach.

_______________________________________Daisy packed her bag and closed it shut.

_______________________________________ They got their umbrella and their picnic bags ready, shut the front door, and loaded everything into the trunk of their car. And _____________________Off they went.

_______________________ Finally, they braked to halt in front of their destination. They quickly changed into their bathing suits, laid out their towels, set up their umbrella, and _________________ They jumped into the water. Daisy had a great weekend at the beach.

DEBATING

Debating is like having a discussion, but in a more organized way with rules. It's a way for people to talk about different ideas or opinions. In a debate, two teams take turns talking about a topic. One team supports the idea, and the other team disagrees. Each team tries to explain their points well and convince everyone that their side is the right one. There are judges who decide which team did the best job. It's a way for people to practice expressing their thoughts and listening to others in a respectful way.

Debate Like a Pro

Topic: The question of whether homework should be abolished?

Moderator: Opening Statement

Greetings, esteemed educators and dear classmates. Today we gather to discuss a topic that directly affects us all: the question of whether homework should be abolished. On one side, Abdur – Rahmaan Jackson advocates for its abolition, while on the flip side, Marika Howell maintains that homework is important.

Debater 1: Hello, everyone! My name is Abdur – Rahmaan Jackson, and I believe that homework should be abolished. Kids work hard at school all day, and when they go home, they need time to relax, play, and spend time with family. Homework takes away from that precious time and can make kids feel stressed. We can learn in many different ways, and we don't always need homework to do that.

Moderator: Thank you, Abdur – Rahmaan Jackson. Now, Marika Howell, your opening statement.

Debater 2: Hi, everyone. I'm Marika Howell, and I think homework is important. It helps us practice what we learned in school and makes sure we really understand the lessons. Homework also teaches us responsibility and time management. If we don't have homework, we might forget what we learned in class. Plus, it gives parents a chance to see what we're working on and help us if we need it.

Moderator: Great opening statements! Now, Abdur – Rahmaan Jackson, present your main argument.

Debater 1: My main argument is that kids need time to be kids. After a long day at school, we should be able to play, relax, and do things we enjoy. Homework takes away that free time and can make us feel too pressured. There are many other ways to learn, like projects and interactive activities in class.

Moderator: Thank you. Marika Howell, your response.

Debater 2: I understand wanting free time, but homework helps us reinforce what we learn. It's like practicing a sport or playing a musical instrument. Without practice, we might forget how to do things. Also, homework helps us become responsible learners, which is important for our future.

Moderator: Well said! Now, Abdur – Rahmaan Jackson, acknowledge a possible counterargument.

Debater 1: I know some people might say that homework prepares us for the future, but there are other ways to learn responsibility and time management. We can do chores, participate in clubs, and still have time for fun activities.

Moderator: Interesting point. Marika Howell, your thoughts on the counterargument?

Debater 2: While those activities are valuable, homework is specifically designed to reinforce what we learn in school. It's like a bridge between school and home, helping us remember and understand things better.

Moderator: Thank you both for your perspectives. Abdur – Rahmaan Jackson, give your rebuttal.

Debater 1: In response, I believe that projects and in class activities are more effective ways to reinforce learning without taking away our free time. Homework can sometimes feel like a burden, and there are better alternatives.

Moderator: Got it. Marika Howell, your final thoughts?

Debater 2: Homework might feel challenging sometimes, but it's a valuable tool for our education. It helps us practice, learn responsibility, and stay connected with what we're studying. Abolishing homework might leave us with gaps in our understanding."
Now, we'll open the floor to questions from the audience.

Activity: Answer the debating questions below.

1. What's your personal experience with homework? Do you find it helpful or challenging, and why?

____

____

____

2. Can you think of other ways, besides homework, that might help us remember and understand what we learn in school?

____

____

3. How do you feel about having more free time after school, and what activities would you enjoy doing during that time?

____

____

____

4. After reading the example debate, did you feel like it showed what a debate is like? If yes, what part did you like the most?

____

____

____

Debate Like a Pro

Topic: Should Students Have a Say in Classroom Rules?

- Arguments for: Encourages responsibility and a sense of ownership.

- Arguments against: Teachers are trained to make rules that benefit everyone.

Instructions:

1. Use the guided prompts to organize your thoughts and make your points strong.

2. Talk confidently so everyone can understand what you're saying.

3. Use examples that matter to you and your friends to explain your points.

4. Be polite and share your ideas without attacking others.

5. Practice what you want to say and get ready for questions.

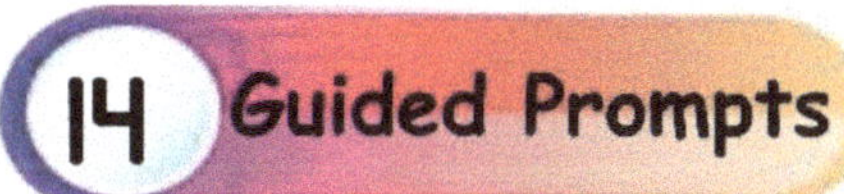

Introduction: Greeting and Opening Statement

1. Begin by greeting the audience and introducing yourself.

2. State the topic of the debate in a clear and concise manner.

Definition of Key Terms:

3 Define any important terms to ensure everyone understands the topic.

Thesis Statement:

4 Tell your reader what you think about the topic. It's like saying, "Here's what I believe or want to talk about."

Body: Main Arguments:

5 Share each of your reasons in a different paragraph. This is where you explain why you have that belief.

6 Back up each reason with proof or examples. Use things like facts or examples to show why you think your idea is true.

Counterarguments:

7 Think about what others might say against your idea.

8 Explain why you still think your idea is the best.

Rebuttal:

9 Answer what others say against your idea.

10 Repeat your main reasons to show why you're right.

Conclusion: Summarize Main Points:

11 Quickly talk about the important reasons you shared.

Closing Statement:

(12) Finish with a strong and easy-to-remember last thing you want to say.

Debate Like a Pro

Topic: Should schools include financial literacy as a subject in their curriculum.

- Arguments for: Financial literacy helps us become better at handling money responsibly.
- kids at this age might find these money topics too difficult to understand, making it harder for them to learn.

Instructions:

1. Read each prompt. Write the example sentences provided below. Afterward, include your own reasons or good points to complete the sentences.
2. Talk confidently so everyone can understand what you're saying.
3. Use examples that matter to you and your friends to explain your points.
4. Be polite and share your ideas without attacking others.
5. Practice what you want to say and get ready for questions.

Introduction: Greeting and Opening Statement

1 **Start by saying,** Hello everyone! My name is [Your Name], and today I'll be talking about [Debate Topic].

Definition of Key Terms

2 **Provide clarity by saying:** Before we dive in, let's make sure we all understand what [Key Term] means. In this debate, [Key Term] refers to [Definition].

Thesis Statement:

3 **Clearly state your position:** I firmly believe that schools [Your Stance] because [Reason 1], [Reason 2], and [Reason 3].

Body: Main Arguments

4 **Present reasons with support:** Reason 1: [State Reason]. It's important because [Explain Reason]. For instance, [Provide Example or Evidence].

Counterarguments

5 **Acknowledge opposing views:** Some might argue [Counterargument], but I disagree because [Explain Why].

Rebuttal

6 Address any counterarguments raised by the opposing side: In response to [Counterargument], it's important to emphasize [Reinforce Your Argument].

Conclusion: Summarize Main Points

7 Recap key points: To sum up, I believe [Your Stance] due to [Reason 1], [Reason 2], and [Reason 3].

Closing Statement

8 End with impact: Thank you for your attention. Let's keep in mind that [Your Stance] is crucial because [Final Thought].

Non - Fiction Narrative

Non-fiction narrative refers to a story or account that is based on real events, facts, and experiences. They can encompass various genres such as memoirs, biographies, autobiographies, essays, travel accounts, and historical writings.

The fisherman

Instruction:

The story is jumbled. Utilize the writing guide sentences to assist you in arranging the story correctly in three paragraphs.

17 Writing Guide

1. Describe the early morning atmosphere as the fisherman begins his day. 1st par.

2. Explain how he prepares himself and pushes his boat into the water.

3. Detail how he sets sail toward the middle of the sea. 2nd par.

4. Express his optimistic thoughts about the fishes in the area.

5. Describe his satisfaction and happiness an hour later. 3rd par.

6. Explain his reason for heading to the market.

Jumbled Story

Satisfied with his catch, he efficiently packed up his belongings and headed straight to the market, where he successfully sold his entire haul. "Many fish gather in this area; today's catch will surely be bountiful," he thought optimistically.

With his net in hand, he gently tossed it into his boat and started pushing the vessel into the water. Setting sail towards the middle of the sea, he skillfully cast his net into the depths of the sea "splash".

An hour passed, and his anticipation transformed into joy as he hauled in a significant number of fish. At the crack of dawn, a determined fisherman prepared for his day on the sea.

The fisherman

At the crack of dawn, a determined fisherman prepared for his day on the sea. With his net in hand, he gently tossed it into his boat and started pushing the vessel into the water.

Setting sail towards the middle of the sea, he skilfully cast his net into the depths of the sea "splash". "Many fish gather in this area; today's catch will surely be bountiful," he thought optimistically.

An hour later, he was so happy with the amount of fish he caught. He packed up and went straight to the market and sold them all.

Activity: Answer the questions

1 Do you believe the context clues were helpful in accurately sequencing the story back into the correct order? Explain your reasoning. ____

____

2 Which word from the story describes how the fisherman throws his net into the sea? ____

____

3 Who is the main character in the story about the fisherman?

____

4 What did the fisherman think about the area he was fishing in?

____

____

National Dance Competition

<u>Instructions:</u>

1. The narrative is jumbled. Utilize the writing guide sentences to assist you in arranging the narrative in the correct order.

2. Use each sentence as a context clue and order them by their numbered sequence provided.

18 Writing Guide

1. Write about how 3 friends received a special invitation.

2. Express their shared passion for dancing.

3. Convey the excitement the friends felt as they prepared for their journey.

4. Write about Kelly's positive suggestion, expressing her optimism.

5. Describe Kelly's Curiosity and Tania's Enthusiastic response to the choreography ideas, capturing their agreement.

6. Mention Kelly's Declaration and Spirit-Boosting Remark.

7. Convey how the trio spent the entire night.

8. Detail how the friends were fully prepared for the competition.

9 Describe the moment when their favorite song started to play.

10 Emphasize their seamless performance on stage.

11 Express the crowd's reaction to their performance.

National Dance Competition

Filled with excitement, they prepared their bags and eagerly embarked on their journey to the event. Their shared passion for dancing made this opportunity even more thrilling.

Three close friends, Maria, Kelly, and Tania, received a special invitation to the prestigious National Dance Competition in Wimbledon.

Maria, curious about their dance routine, inquired, "What moves are we planning?" Tania, full of enthusiasm, replied, "I have some choreography ideas. Want to see?" Excitedly Kelly and Maria agreed.

"Maybe we're here to replace the team that dropped out," Kelly suggest suggested optimistically. The trio spent the entire night in the dance studio, practicing their routines, observing each other's moves, and mastering the choreography. "Let's pray and prepare to win this contest!" Kelly declared, boosting their spirits.

Without missing a beat, they danced in perfect harmony, captivating the audience from the very beginning. When the competition day arrived, they were fully prepared. The crowd cheered as they Executed their routine,

showcasing their talent and dedication. With their favorite song playing in the background and hearts pounding with anticipation, the three friends confidently took the stage.

Activity: Read questions and circle the correct answer.

1 What category this story falls under?

A) Fiction

B) Non-Fiction

C) Biography

2 What was the special event that Maria, Kelly, and Tania were invited to?

A) National Dance Competition

B) Wimbledon Tennis Tournament

C) Music Concert

3 Did the context clues help order the story correctly, yes or no?

A Trip to Kenya

<u>Instructions:</u>

1. The story is jumbled. Utilize the writing guide sentences to assist you in arranging the story in the correct order.

2. Use each sentence as a context clue and order them by their numbered sequence provided.

19 Writing Guide

Introduce the Setting and Characters: 1st Par.

1 Describe the significance of summer as a vacation time, introduce the Grizwold family and their decision to travel to Kenya.

2 Explain Janie and Jeff's initial reaction when they first heard about the trip.

3 Why were they excited about exploring Africa, and what intrigued them about it?

Conveying the Jungle Experience: 2nd Par.

4 What unexpected thing did Janie and Jeff encounter when they arrived in the Kenyan jungle?

5 Describe the difference between their expectations and what they actually found there, including the unique appearance of the local woman who greeted them.

Compare Expectations with Reality: 3rd Par.

6 What was special about the jungle for the local tribe? How did the tribe get what they needed to live?

7 Share Janie and Jeff's thoughts about the tribe's way of life.

8 Capture the Grizworld kids' reaction as they witness the tribe worked together as a team in their community.

Showcase Learning and Cultural Exchange: 4th Par.

9 Describe Janie and Jeff's active involvement in the tribe's lifestyle over the following week

10 Detail the practical skills acquired by Janie and Jeff.

11 Highlight how these skills learned by Janie and Jeff went beyond traditional classroom education.

Transition to Village Life: 5th Par.

12 Describe their move to the nearby village, elaborating on their living conditions.

13 Convey their interactions with the local woman and how she guides them through essential tasks.

(14) Highlight the family's enthusiasm as they help prepare dinner by the fireside and integrate into the tribe's everyday activities.

15 Capture the special learning experience of their journey, showcasing a side of life that's completely different from what they knew in the city.

A Trip to Kenya

Africa held so much mystery for them, and they couldn't wait to explore. Janie and Jeff were really excited. Summer had always been the perfect time for family vacations, and this year, the Grizworld family decided to embark on an extraordinary journey to Kenya.

Instead of fancy safaris and tourist scenes they'd seen in movies, they found themselves greeted by a local woman adorned with tattoos and piercings, a sight unlike anything they had ever seen before. When they reached the Kenyan jungle, they were in for a surprise.

They saw how everyone worked together and learned important lessons about teamwork and living with nature. It provided everything the local tribe needed to survive.

The jungle was amazing in its own way. Janie and Jeff found the tribe's way of life very interesting.

These were lessons that extended far beyond any classroom, teaching them resilienceand resourcefulness they wouldn't have gained back in the city. They learned how to hunt, fish, and cook over an open fire. During the week, Janie and Jeff got involved in the tribe's daily activities.

It was an adventure they'd never forget, it showed them a different way of life than what they knew in the city. Later, the Grizworld family moved to a nearby village.

With the help of the friendly local lady, they discovered where to gather water and where to find the restroom. They stayed in a simple hut with beds made from sticks. They even helped with preparing meals over a fire, just like the tribe.

Fiction Narratives

A fiction narrative is a story that is created from the imagination rather than being based on real-life events. In fiction narratives, authors invent characters, settings, and events to entertain, inspire, or convey a message to the readers.

The Protest

<u>Instructions:</u>

1. Rewrite the story, change the characters to animals that create similar food.

2. Replace the underlined words with synonyms to make the narrative more engaging.

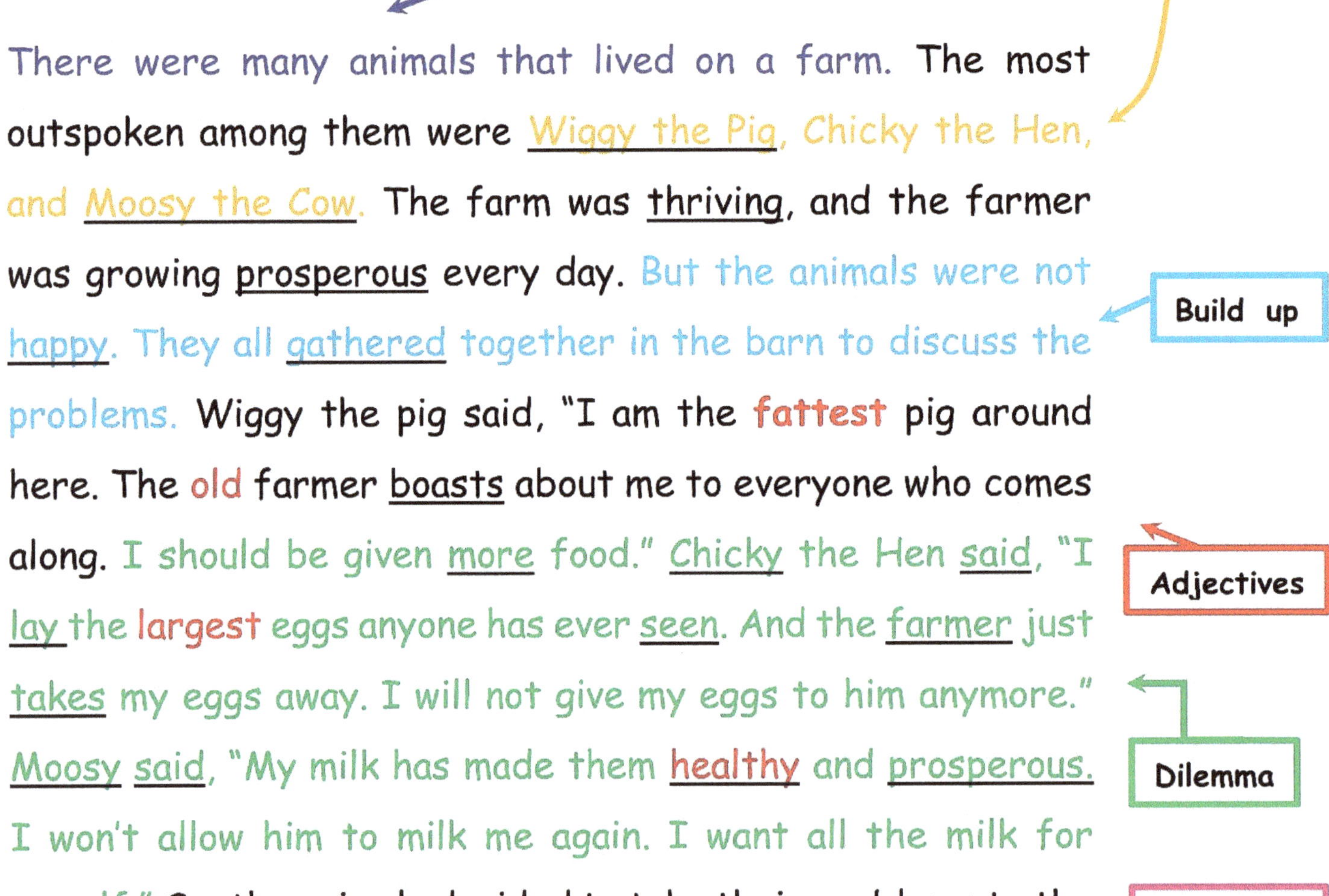

farmer. The old farmer listened patiently. He smiled and said, "As you wish!" So, the pig was given more food and finally, he couldn't move at all. The farmer stopped taking the eggs from the hen's coop. They piled up and broke whenever the hen tried to move. The broken shells hurt her. The farmer stopped milking the cow and slowly, the milk accumulated in her body. It caused a painful infection. The animals understood their mistake and apologized to the farmer. The farmer started taking care of them again.

The Tiger's Friend

<u>Instructions:</u>

1. Rewrite the story about the Rabbit's Friend.

2. Change the characters and the title of the story.

3. Replace the underlined words with synonyms.

Story

Bunny, the <u>funny</u> rabbit, <u>strolled</u> through the <u>forest</u>, crossing the babbling brook and the <u>prickly</u> <u>shrubs</u>. Before he knew it, he found himself <u>deep</u> in the <u>jungle</u>.

"Hold on! Did I hear something?" he <u>whispered</u> to himself. There was a <u>rustle</u> of <u>leaves</u>, a <u>hustle</u> of <u>birds</u>, and a <u>deafening</u> <u>roar</u>! "ROAAAAARRRRR!" It was Marumba, the <u>mightiest</u> lion in the <u>jungle</u>.
"Where are you off to, Mr. Bunny?" Marumba <u>inquired</u>. "I'm <u>famished</u> and in need of a good meal," he <u>confessed</u>.

Bunny felt a <u>shiver</u> down his <u>spine</u>, but his mind was <u>sharp</u>. "Well, Mr. Lion, you see, I'm on my way to a <u>pal's</u> place. If I don't show up, he might come <u>searching</u> for me." "Oh, and who might this friend be?" asked the <u>hungry</u> lion. "He's a grizzalion," the rabbit replied. "He has <u>shaggy</u> <u>black</u> fur, long, <u>pointed</u> claws, and a head as <u>enormous</u> as a <u>car</u>. Even from the <u>moon</u>, you can hear him <u>burp</u>."

The lion <u>quivered</u> in fear. "I'd rather not end up as someone's <u>dinner</u>, especially not a grizzalion's! Please, go ahead. <u>Hurry</u> to your friend's house," the lion <u>urged</u>. So, Bunny <u>continued</u> his journey, eventually returning <u>safely</u> to his home. "What a <u>gullible</u> lion," he <u>chuckled</u>. "Is there even such a thing as a grizzalion?"

Activity:

1. How does Bunny initially feel when he encounters Marumba in the jungle?

____

____

2. What clever excuse does Bunny come up with to avoid becoming Marumba's meal? ______________________________

____

3. How does Marumba react when Bunny mentions the grizzalion?

____

____

4. What did Bunny think about Marumba after he safely returned home?

____

____

____

The Ant in The Ditch

Instructions:

1. Rewrite the narrative of "The Ant in the Ditch."
2. Substitute the words and phrases underlined in black with something comparable or contrasting.
3. Replace the words underlined in pink with synonyms.
4. Write your own conclusion for the narrative.

In a dense forest, there was an anthill. It was home to a colony of ants. Every year, the rain washed away the ant hill. So, the ant queen ordered the worker ants to build a shed over the ant hill. She also wanted a trench around the ditch.

The worker ants set to work with great fervor. One day, it was raining heavily. While working, one of the ants slipped and fell into a deep ditch near the anthill. The ant was badly hurt. But he was determined to come out. The ditch was slippery from the rain and the ant kept slipping down. But he did not give up. "I must keep trying," the ant told himself.

Sensory Story Writing

Sensory story writing involves using vivid descriptions that appeal to the five senses: sight, sound, smell, taste, and touch. It includes using words that create a sensory experience, enabling the reader to imagine and feel the story more deeply.

Intruder in the Night

> **Definition:** **Sensory language** means using words that describe things you can see, hear, smell, taste, and touch.
>
> **Examples: Touch:** The kitten's fur felt soft and fluffy.

Instructions:

Examine the picture and utilize the table containing vocabulary and the five senses below to draft your story before you begin writing.

Vocabulary	Describe the character's experience using vivid adjectives that depict what was seen, felt, smelled, heard, and tasted.
Creaking	**Sight:** bright flash of lightning, shadow of a figure, crooked nose, long horns.
Whistling	
Rustled	
Parched	
Thumping	
Bright	**Sound:** creaking of the wooden floorboard, wind whistling, drying leaves rustled, loud rumble of thunder, shattering of glass.
Deafened	
Blinded	
Crooked	
Long, slowly	
Peculiar	**Smell:** peculiar, faintly foul odor of dampness.
Faintly foul	
Dry	
Rasping	**Taste:** dry taste lingering.
Loud, strong	
Shattering	**Touch:** feeling the thumping of her own heartbeat, all that came out was a rasping sound.

Intruder in the Night

Alice was asleep in her bedroom when was woken by a **creaking of the wooden floorboard**. There was someone inside their house! She could also **hear the wind whistling** through the open window. The drying leaves of the old oak tree outside her window **rustled in the strong wind**.

Her throat was parched, leaving a dry taste lingering and she could **feel the thumping of her own heartbeat**.

She tiptoed to her door and slowly peeked outside. Just then, there was a **bright flash of lightning**. Alice was deafened by the **loud rumble of thunder** and blinded by the sudden flash of light. As she blinked, she saw the shadow of a figure right next to the corridor window.

It had a crooked nose and long horns, emanating a peculiar, faintly foul odor of dampness lingering in the air.

Alice shrieked aloud in fear, but all that came out was a rasping sound. Almost immediately, there was a **shattering of the glass** as the crooked figure flew out of the window.

Activity:

1. What woke Alice up from her sleep? _______________________

____

2. What did Alice see outside her window during the storm?

____

____

3. How do you think Alice felt when she saw the shadowy figure?

____

4. What did the figure do after Alice screamed? _______________

____

Whispers in the Forest

Instructions:

Utilize the table containing vocabulary and the five senses below to draft your story before you begin writing.

Vocabulary	Describe the experiences of the characters using vivid adjectives that describe what they
enchanted	Sight:
tranquil	
Harmonize	
calm	
swiftly	
softly	
dejected	
Joyful	Sound:
chirp	
slimy	
soft	
earthy	Smell:
Scorching	
shaggy	
woody	
musty	
melodic	Taste:
whisper	
melancholic	
Hugh	
Sad	
Serene	Touch:
subtle	

Ms. Penn's Everyday Chronicles

Instructions:

Utilize the table containing vocabulary and the five senses below to draft your story before you begin writing.

Vocabulary	Describe the experiences of the characters using vivid adjectives that describe what they 👆 👀 👂 👃 👅
Bright	Sight:
Neatly	
Chopping	
Soft	
Clean	
Steamy	
Humming	
Fragrant	Sound:
Crisp	
Smooth	
Fresh	
Simmering	Smell:
Vibrant	
Aromatic	
Savory	
Smooth	
Satisfying	Taste:
Sizzling	
Swishing	
Flavorful	
Silken	
Whirling	Touch:
decorum	

Let's Write to Persuade

Persuasive writing is when you try to convince others to agree with your ideas or opinions.

A Puppy for my Birthday

Introduction
Start with a question or an interesting statement

Argument 1
State your opinion or what you want from the other person

Argument 2
State a reason to support your point

Argument 3
Use linking words such as because, Also, another or moreover etc.

Argument 4
Try to include facts that support your point of view

Conclusion
End the passage with a convincing line. Encourage the person to act upon your request.

Why I should be gifted with a puppy for my birthday

Did you know, children with pets, grow up to be kind and gentle?

Please get me a puppy for my birthday.

A puppy will be a great companion for me when you are at work.

Also, we can go to the playground together. **Moreover,** taking the puppy for a walk everyday will help me stay fit.

Another benefit of taking care of the puppy is that it will make me responsible.

It is well known that children with pets are more creative and social.

I promise not to watch TV if you get me a puppy.

Asking Parents for Pocket Money

Introduction
Start with a question or an interesting statement

Argument 1
State your opinion or what you want from the other person

Argument 2
State a reason to support your point

Argument 3
Use linking words such as because, Also, another or moreover etc.

Argument 4
Try to include facts that support your point of view

Conclusion
End the passage with a convincing line. Encourage the person to act upon your request.

Dear ______________

I firmly believe that children who are expose to money at an early age are better at managing it in their early life.

____

____

____

____

It could be argued that exposing children to pocket money at an early age might cause them to become obsessed with it, hence dropping out of school to get a job.

____

____

____

____

____

____

We Should Plant More Trees

Introduction

Did you know that if trees are cut down, a place can soon become a desert?

We must plant more trees for a cleaner environment.

linking words

(research 1)
Trees are important because

(research 2)
trees also

(research 3)
moreover,

counter argument

convincing line

(research fact)
If all trees are cut down

Conclusion

Hence, we must plant more trees

Asking Classmates to Vote for You

to Become Class President

Practice

Introduction

linking words

{ **counter argument** }

[**convincing line**]

Conclusion

Advertising

Advertising is like the way companies and businesses tell people about their products or services. You see ads everywhere, on TV, the internet, billboards, and even in magazines. But have you ever wondered why they're everywhere? Well, that's because advertising helps businesses let people know about the cool things they have to offer!

Advertising Guide

Creating an Exciting Product Description:

✔ Exciting Name: Choose a name that reflects what your product is all about.

✔ Purpose: Describe what your product is for (e.g., exploration, art, science).

✔ Benefits: Briefly describe what it offers or enables persons to do, making it sound like an engaging story to grab everyone's interest.

What sets your product apart?

✔ Share 3 specific details about your product that make it different from others in the same category. For instance, texture, size, positive feedback, etc.

How will your product stand out from competitors?

✔ E.g. The product packaging, the extra items that come with your product etc.

Why should people buy your products?

✔ Describe the benefits & features. E.g long lasting, durable, reusable etc.

Who will your customers be – kids, woman, or men

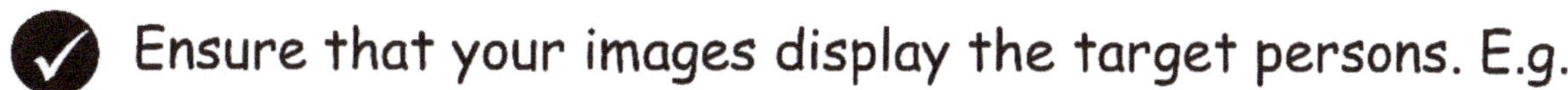 Ensure that your images display the target persons. E.g.

Kids - your images should be kids friendly and have clear information.

Include product images that depict what the product looks like.

E.g. Appealing pictures showcasing a colorful art set with paints, brushes, and sketchbooks.

Description: Express how this product helps unleash your artistic skills!

Ensure to include the cost of your product.

E.g. $29.99

COLORCRAFT SMARTPEN

Your Art, Your Rules!

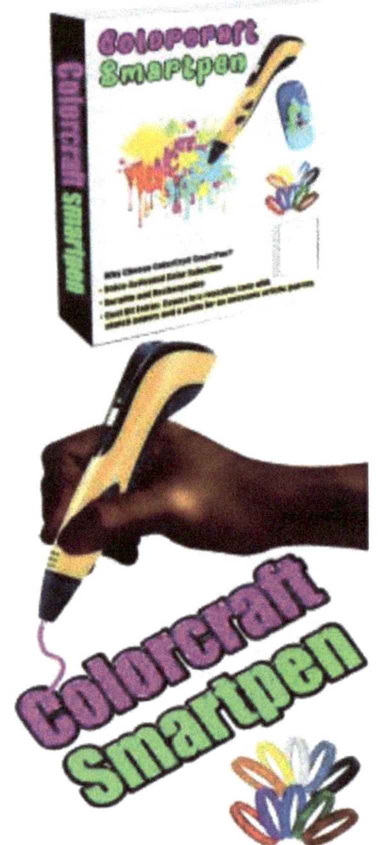

🚀 **Product Description:**

ColorCraft SmartPen transforms your ideas into vibrant, personalized masterpieces with voice-activated color and font selection.

✨ **Discover what sets our product apart!**

☀ **Comfortable Design:** Ergonomic and perfect for children, ensuring a magical grip.

✏ **Compact Power:** Advanced technology in a portable size for creativity anywhere.

🐚 **Rave Reviews:** Turn ordinary drawings into eye-catching creations.

Standing Out in the World of Color:

🎁 **Cool Kit Extras:** Reusable case, sketch papers, and an art guide.

🐚 **Eco-Friendly Package:** Reusable packaging for your creative adventures.

✴ **Why Choose ColorCraft SmartPen?**

💡 **Voice-Activated Color:** Effortlessly infuse exact colors into your drawings.

✂ **Durable & Rechargeable:** Long-lasting and rechargeable for continuous creativity.

✴ **Your Art, Your Style:** Easily switch between fonts and styles for unique creations.

👥 **For Creative Minds for Ages 5+:**
Designed for young artists to elevate their drawings with vibrant colors!

Ready to Make Your Art Magical?
Visit ColorCraft SmartPen.com or call 18767818571 to get your ColorCraft SmartPen now! Limited stock available! **Cost only $29.99**

Product Review Questions

<u>Instructions</u>

Share your honest thoughts on the product using details from the flyer and image to assist others in deciding if the product suits them.

Review Questions:

1. **Product Appeal:** Based on its visual representation in the flyer, what aspects of the ColorCraft SmartPen catch your attention the most?

____

____

2. **Design and Size:** From the image, how does the pen's design look to you? Does it seem comfortable to hold and use? Explain your response.

____

____

____

3. **Additional Features:** What are your thoughts on the extra items mentioned like the reusable case, sketch papers, and art guide? Do they add value to the overall product? If yes, why?

____

____

____

4 **Functionality:** How does the idea of selecting colors and fonts with your voice appeal to you?

____

____

5 Do you think this feature would make drawing more enjoyable or convenient?

____

____

Critique Questions:

6 **Clarity of Information:** Were you able to understand all the details mentioned in the flyer about the ColorCraft SmartPen? Is there anything that was unclear or confusing?

____

____

7 **Imagery Impact:** Do you think the images used effectively showcase what the product does?

____

____

8 Are there any additional images or details you would like to see to better understand the product?

____

____

____

9 **Comparative Analysis:** How does this pen seem different from other pens or art tools you've used before?

____

____

____

10 What makes it stand out or what could be improved to make it more unique?

____

____

____

11 **Pricing and Affordability:** What do you think about the price of the ColorCraft SmartPen based on its features?

Do you feel it's a fair price for what it offers?

____

____

____

12 **User Reviews and Ratings:** What do other users, particularly parents and friends, say about the smart pen?

____

____

Advertising Guide

Instructions

Create a captivating flyer for your product using this guide. Choose a legal-size cardstock paper in your preferred color. Design an engaging flyer that effectively showcases all eight points outlined in the guide, and use it to inform everyone about your fantastic product.

1 **Product Name:**
- Start by giving your product a fun name that tells audience what it's all about.
- Briefly describes what the product offers or allows kids to do.

2 **Unique Features:**
- Highlight three standout features that make the product different from others in the same category.
- This could include durability, size, special accessories, interactive elements, or educational benefits.

3 **Standout Qualities:**
- Describe how your product stands out from competitors. Focus on aspects like unique packaging, bonus items, interactive components, or any special additions that make it extra exciting.

4 Benefits and Features:

- Explain why kids should choose this product. Emphasize its benefits, such as educational value, fun activities, durability, portability, or how it encourages creativity and exploration.

5 Target Audience:

- Clearly identify the intended audience, whether it's kids aged 9-12, creative minds, or anyone passionate about a specific hobby or interest.

6 Product Cost:

- Include the price of the product.
- Make sure it's clear and visible within the description.

7 Images:

- Use captivating images that showcase the product in action or being used by kids in a fun and engaging way.
- Ensure the images align with the target audience and clearly display what the product looks like.

8 Call-to-Action (CTA):

- Encourage kids to take action! Use an engaging CTA that prompts them to explore, discover, or buy the product.
- For example, Start your adventure today by………

Poems

Poems are like magic words that come together to create something beautiful. They're a special kind of writing that uses rhythm, sound, and imagery to express feelings, ideas, or tell a story in a unique way. Poems come in all shapes and sizes - some are short and simple, while others are long and complex.

Rhyming Poems

<u>Instructions:</u>

Choose the most suitable rhyming word to complete the poem.

A penny in my pocket

In my _____________________ (pocket/jelly), it was somewhat smelly

So, I took it to the _____________________ (deli/store), they said go to the belly.

Of the town of _____________________ (City/<u>Delhi</u>) I went there in a frenzy

But the wind was _____________________ (heavy, slow), the man said, "Hey, this is somewhat smelly,

Let me wash it in some _____________________ (jelly/water), it made me very merry

That my penny was now _____________________ (ready/new)

To be given to my teddy.

Acrostic Peom

Note: Acrostic poems are simple poems in which the first letter of each line spells out a word or phrase.

Instructions:

1. Read the example below.

2. Use your first and last name to create an acrostic poem below.

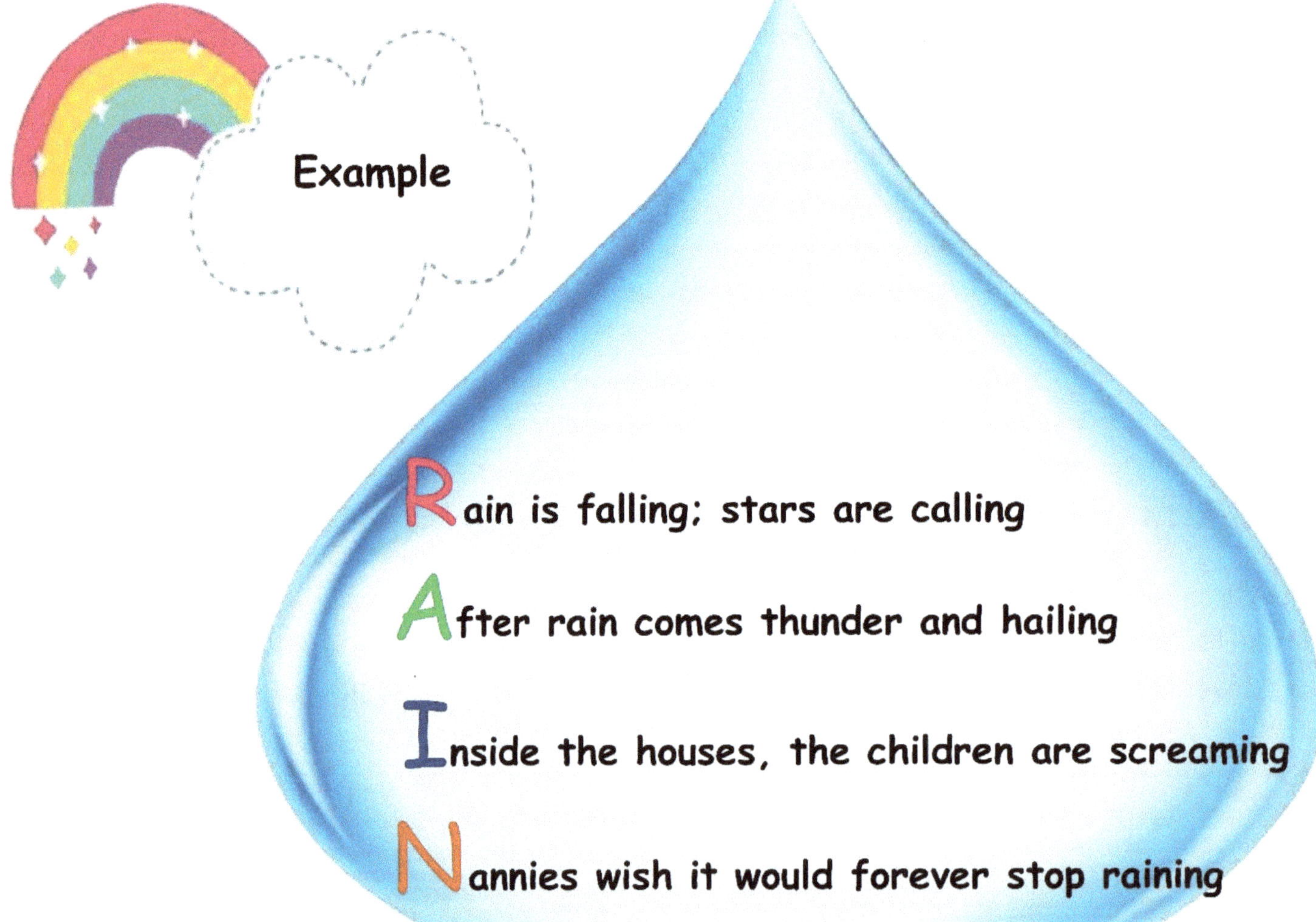

Grammar Poem

Instructions: Complete the poem using the hints as a guide.

There was once a/an _________________________ (adjective)

_____________________ (noun person/animal)

from _____________________ (noun place).

Whose _______________________(noun, feature like nose)

was/were _______________________(-ly adverb)

_________________(adjective).

He/She/It _________________(something that happened).

And _________________ (more details of the story).

To me he/she/it was _________________ (-ly adverb)

_________________ (adjective).

We used to _____________________ (verb)

every day in the _______________________ (noun place).

We ate snacks at _______________________(adverb time) every day.

Now, he/she/it must be _________________ (-ing verb)

in the _________________ (noun place).

That _________________ (adjective from first line) _________________

(noun from second line) from _______________________ (place from third

line).

Rhyming Peom

<u>Instructions:</u>

Write your own rhyming poem.

Topic and Due Date   Page no.

Notes/ Comments